GW00375219

All rights reserved; no part of this book may be reproduced, stored in a retrieval system, or transmitted, in any form or by any means, without the prior permission in writing from the publisher, nor be otherwise circulated in any form of binding or cover other than that in which it is published and without a similar condition including this condition being imposed on the subsequent purchaser.

First published in Great Britain in 2008 by Helen Astrid
Second Edition published in Great Britain in 2013 by Helen Astrid

Copyright © 2008 Helen Astrid
The moral right of the author has been asserted.

ISBN: 978-1492886211

The suggestions in this book are not to be substituted for medical or professional attention. Any application of these tips is at the reader's sole discretion and risk.

Singing Tips at your Fingertips

Transform and Empower your Voice

Helen Astrid

Reviews for Singing Tips:

"For the beginner or seasoned professional, Helen Astrid's Singing Tips at your Fingertips is concise and informative. If you want to aim for the Grammys or merely knock 'em dead at your local karaoke bar, this short, knowledgeable and very readable book can help you get started. The technical advice is geared toward practical results e.g. how to give a successful audition, but the real aim is to unlock the singer within. Singing in front of an audience is always a challenge, and half the battle is building up self-confidence. This will help you do that, and the rewards can enrich your life in other ways too. The anecdotes remind us that the pros need just as much help as anyone else. One place to find it is here."

Gary Lachman reviews for the Guardian and Independent on Sunday. As Gary Valentine he was a founding member of Blondie, and a guitarist with Iggy Pop. Along with Debbie Harry, his songs have been recorded by Annie Lennox and Tracy Ullman.

"Singing Tips at your Fingertips answer so many questions I have long wanted to ask. This book is a goldmine." *Michael Nealon, bass chorister*

"There are lots of valuable tips here and I like the fact I can start anywhere and improve straight away. It's light and thoughtful, two qualities that are difficult to put together. Above all, it's for everyone." *Christine Jaeck-Janet, Cyberlibris publishing*

"It's good, educational and lots of fun." *David Harman, proof-reader, editor*

"I'm thrilled that my singing practice is more consistent now. This book keeps me motivated." *Beverley McKeown, soprano soloist*

"I think it's smart to have various tips divided into the seasons. There's something for everyone, regardless of their singing ability. An audio version will be tremendous. Bravo." *Rod Janssen, energy consultant*

"If you're lucky enough to be reading this at the start of your journey as a singer, you'll acquire with ease an understanding that would otherwise have been arduous and hard-earned. Why hasn't someone given me this advice earlier? Quirky, down to earth and far-reaching, Helen is someone who knows how much is involved in the process." *Esther Parkes, singer-songwriter*

Foreword from the Author

I believe there's no such thing as tone-deafness. Everyone can sing, given the chance. It's a question of developing the belief that you can do it and having some helpful tips to support you along the way. There's no reason why you can't learn to sing; singing can be learned at any age.

It's never too late to realise your dream.

I've interspersed facts with quotes from famous people which all helps to unleash and transform your voice to its greatest potential, giving you a tip every day of the year.

About the Author

Helen Astrid is in high demand as a singing coach and has helped thousands of individuals and organisations successfully reach their singing goals. She launched **The Helen Astrid Singing Academy** in London in 2001 and receives substantial press coverage for her work with regular broadcasts on radio and television, including BBC1 News, The Paul O'Grady Show and What the Butler Saw, both for Channel 4.

She was awarded a Scholarship to study at the Royal Academy of Music and gained her Diploma in 1988, presented by Diana, Princess of Wales. She then pursued a career as a soprano soloist at most of the major U.K. music venues including English National Opera, Royal Opera House, Garsington Opera and the South Bank.

Helen was born in Kingston-upon-Thames and educated in Kew and Richmond, Surrey. She is married with two divine cats.

www.singingtipsatyourfingertips.com

www.thehelenastridsingingacademy.com

Acknowledgements

It is with deep gratitude that this book has been made possible by the support, encouragement and ongoing generosity of David Harman, Beverley McKeown and my husband Hor.

Contents

"The high note is not the only thing." Placido Domingo

Spring

Includes breathing tips and postural tips

General Singing Tips

1   A good way to start afresh is to take up a new hobby. Singing is a great hobby and it's free.

2   If you unleash your voice, you'll unleash the real you.

3   You don't need to be able to read music in order to sing beautifully.

4   People generally feel happier when Spring arrives, so it's natural for us to smile more as the weather gets warmer. Sing as if you're smiling, this will help to lift the tone of your voice and make you sound more appealing.

5   Singing is a great way to overcome inhibitions. By letting go, you immediately show that you are confident.

6   When doing vocal exercises, try to feel the vibrations in your body and face and remember that sensation. When it feels good, the sound will be right.

7   If you practise singing at least every other day, it'll keep your voice flexible. Like any muscle, the voice shrinks if it's not used.

8   Just remember that your voice is the only instrument that presents no physical barriers. It's you!

9   What does *messa di voce* mean? This is Italian for 'placing the voice'. It implies that a singer is able to sing from crescendo to decrescendo over a whole range with no breaks or interruptions in the voice.

10 Did you know that there are two separate parts of the brain which govern speech and singing? These are located at different points. If the ability to speak has been lost, singing is still possible, and vice versa.

11 Singers can often be charismatic on stage while being shy and introverted socially.

12 How much practice should you do? I suggest three times a week for approximately half an hour each. It involves being disciplined and focusing on technical exercises, as well as songs and knowing what you're trying to achieve.

13 Your voice undoubtedly reflects your whole personality. When we sing we reveal things about ourselves which we can't hide.

14 If you're hosting a party, you need to take control and ensure all your guests are enjoying themselves. Singing

is much the same; seize the moment and don't shy away.

15   The following determines how your voice sounds: your facial structure, the bones in your face and head, the size and condition of your sinus cavities, the size of your mouth, the arch and elasticity of your soft palate, and finally, the size and condition of your vocal cords.

16   What is the larynx? It's also known as the 'voice box' or 'Adam's apple' and is made of cartilage, like your ear. It's quite resilient but your two vocal cords inside the larynx must be looked after and cared for.

17   What is *vibrato*? When we sing, nerve impulses are transmitted to the muscles of the larynx, causing a rapid fluctuation of tone called *vibrato*. Most opera singers use this.

18   To help with your tuning, ensure that you can hear in your head the exact pitch you're about to sing. This will 'place' the voice correctly.

19   Did you know that singing can help stroke victims? By listening to singing for up to two hours a day, functions in the brain start to normalise and speed up recovery.

20   A famous British singer called Isobel Baillie (1895–1983) said, "Never sing louder than lovely."

21   It's important to keep your teeth in top condition. It will help your consonants.

22   Try and get as much sleep as possible. This will help your voice, especially if you're performing.

23 What is the 'mask' in singing? It's the area in the cheekbones, forehead and nose where part of the voice resonates. Tones placed here have brilliance and ping to them known as '*squillo*'.

24 As you mature, your voice will naturally change. You might find the tone becomes richer and darker.

25 If you sing heavy rock music you might lose the ability to sing falsetto, so be careful!

26 Try not to make an extra vowel sound with words that end with a 'y', such as 'day'. It's best to stretch out the first sound.

27 One of the most challenging aspects of singing is to keep the tone as smooth as possible. By using your body properly, you'll have a better chance of achieving this.

28 Avoid dairy products just before singing, as it coats your vocal cords with mucus and can make you want to cough or clear your throat.

29 Try not to hide from top notes. If you imagine approaching each note from above, it can help.

30 It takes about 10,000 times before a muscle gets used to doing something different. Keep practising your singing as your voice needs exercise.

31 It's not necessary to play a musical instrument in order to sing.

32 Imagine putting the vowels before the consonant. A great tip for *legato* singing!

33   Keep your neck supple and free and try not to lean forwards or backwards.

34   Make sure you have some time off from your singing; your voice needs rest too.

35   As you sing up, think about the notes floating out through the top of your skull. This is when you're able to sing high using the head voice, as if you're literally floating above the notes.

36   The higher up you sing, the more likely you'll feel vibrations in your head or behind the eyes.

37   Both ascending and descending exercises are equally important. Practise both, even if one feels easier than the other.

38   When you sing in front of an audience, you're very exposed. The thought of it can make one extremely vulnerable. The art is in hiding this vulnerability so we appear to ooze confidence. Some acting training would be a worthwhile investment.

39   Why do singers swallow just before singing? This allows the larynx to drop down to a comfortable position.

40   Becoming a singer can be a painful process of realising your strengths and weaknesses.

41   There are no short cuts to learning to sing. Be patient and, most of all, enjoy yourself.

42   "The trees that are slow to grow bear the best fruit."
Molière

43   Listening to music boosts your immune system and makes you feel good.

44   When starting singing lessons, don't worry about what type of singer you'll be. This can take time. Enjoy the journey and experimenting with different styles.

45   Did you know your vocal cords vibrate 55 times per second when singing a low note, and this increases to 1,047 when singing a high note?

46   People who say they're tone-deaf have usually experienced discouragement at an early age. This will cause them to lose confidence in their hearing and they may label themselves as tone-deaf. I believe it's possible to change this.

47   Everyone has to start at the beginning so don't be embarrassed by your lack of experience.

48   Some anti-histamines can be harmful for the voice. If you know you suffer from hay fever, avoid open places where there may be lots of pollen flying around.

49   Hay fever sufferers may find their breathing becomes heavier than usual. Practise taking in slow deep breaths. If you need to take an extra breath for singing, do.

50   When learning a new song, clap out the rhythm first and then speak it in the correct time to the music. Don't try and do everything at once.

51   It's a good discipline to practise your songs without any musical accompaniment. In other words, *a cappella*. It'll make you listen more.

52   Don't worry about the dynamics in your songs. Just sing it out to a vocalise to start with and put the detail in later.

53   What is a 'vocalise'? It is a singing exercise using various vowel sounds to develop flexibility and control of pitch and tone.

54   If you belong to a choir or singing group, remember not to 'push' your voice. It's difficult to know exactly what you sound like amongst lots of other people but, whatever you do, avoid straining your voice.

55   Remember that whatever voice category you fit into, whether a soprano, mezzo-soprano, tenor, baritone or bass, you should have a full range which includes both high and low notes.

56   Humming is a great warm-up exercise as it doesn't tire out your voice.

57   The most important factors to consider when singing are pitching, also known as singing in tune or intonation, beauty of vowels, deep breathing, having an expressive voice and of course, having fun.

Breathing Tips

58   Remember to sing with an open throat. The best way to achieve this is by breathing as if you're about to yawn. This lifts the soft palate and opens the throat at the back.

59   Did you know that singing strengthens the respiratory muscles and can help asthmatics breathe more easily?

60   When inhaling, imagine expanding your ribs as far away from you as possible.

61   Singing will increase your mental alertness as you'll be taking in more oxygen.

62   Make sure you take a long deep breath before you start to sing. Sometimes this can take at least one whole bar before singing.

63   When you've taken your breath, don't hold it - sing!

64   Did you know that your vocal cords can't stretch properly if you smoke? Without the ability to stretch, you can't sing high notes. So quit smoking!

65   By relaxing your knees you'll relax the stomach muscles. Then you'll be able to breathe properly and ultimately, sound better!

66   Your intercostal muscles are situated between the ribs and we use them when we inhale and exhale.

67   Your breath should fill the bottom of your lungs whilst the diaphragm moves down, giving a slight forward movement just above the waist; the ribs move out sideways using the intercostal muscles. When you exhale, the breath should always be controlled, never letting the ribs collapse.

68   Doing a work-out at your local gym isn't going to strengthen your diaphragm for singing. You need to vocalise daily.

69   Your diaphragm has several other functions apart from supporting your breath in singing; it's used when we speak, laugh, cry, go to the toilet and give birth.

70   Your voice is essentially a wind instrument as it requires air to make it sound. The very act of deep breathing helps get more oxygen to our brain and muscles, which in itself induces relaxation.

71   Be careful when you come to the end of a phrase and you're running out of breath. Try not to collapse. Aim to lift up your chest which should give you extra mileage.

72   The following is a useful exercise to extend your breath: inhale as deeply as possible, then sing on a low monotone (the same note) 'moo-ee' (without rushing) 'yah', holding the 'yah' for as long as possible. Keep it fairly quiet and support your breath as much as you can by pulling your stomach inwards. See how many seconds you can last. Try to increase your count each time.

73   Lie down on a comfortable flat surface and place a large book on your abdomen. When you take in a deep breath, keep your ribcage expanded as much as possible and try not to let the book drop down when you exhale.

74   A good way to extend your breath is to inhale as normal, then slowly exhale keeping your ribcage expanded. Don't collapse. As you exhale, count to ten to start with and try to increase the count each time.

Postural Tips

75   Singing involves the whole body, not just from the neck upwards. Have a good stretch before you start to sing, then check your posture. Open your chest and

shoulders; relax your knees and tummy. Now you're ready to begin.

76 Singing will improve your posture, which will affect every aspect of your life.

77 Never feel you have to stand rigidly; allow yourself to move freely.

78 Ensure your weight is evenly balanced on both feet, as this will reflect in your singing voice.

79 Keep the back of your tongue relaxed, otherwise it could be an obstacle and block your sound. Try and keep it forwards when singing.

80 If you don't have a singing teacher, look in a mirror or get a video camera and film yourself. Any bad postural habits will be more obvious.

81 The voice has three main zones of resonance, the head, mouth and throat. To achieve a balanced tone, you must use all of these.

82 Practise singing lying on the floor. This will support your back and may even seem easier. When you stand up to sing, imagine being supported from behind.

83 Keep your shoulders down when singing!

84 Don't forget, we were originally designed to sing not speak.

85 Stand with your pelvis tilted slightly forwards and at the same time, clench your buttocks. This will give you a stronger position for singing.

86   Many people find the Alexander Technique useful in correcting any postural problems. Again, this should also improve your voice.

87   When you sing in your middle range, try and feel the vibrations in your chest. You should feel a sort of buzzing sensation.

88   Pilates, yoga and swimming are excellent activities for singers.

"Slow down, you're doing fine. You can't be everything you want to be before your time." Billy Joel

Summer

Includes health tips and karaoke tips

General Singing Tips

89 The art of beautiful singing derives from the term '*bel canto*', meaning 'beautiful song'. This began during the 17th century, when the emphasis was on vocal flexibility. Composers that best exemplify this are Rossini (1792–1868), Bellini (1801–35) and Donizetti (1797–1848).

90 Why are Italians such good singers? Going back hundreds of years, they would train their voices every day and sing outside in the warm sunshine. Lifestyle and environment have a huge impact on your voice.

91 The way we speak can affect the way we sing, e.g. Italians have a bright twang in their sound which is ideal for singing.

92   Italian is a wonderful language for singing because of the beautiful open vowel sounds.

93   When you perform in a foreign language, ensure that you understand every word. And do read through your song with a native speaker before you sing it in public.

94   Singing in another language is good for training your musical ear.

95   The OO vowel is great to practise as it opens up the throat, which is essential for good singing.

96   The EE vowel is excellent for strengthening the falsetto.

97   Gentle physical stretches e.g. reaching as high as you can with both hands above your head, are an excellent warm-up exercise before singing.

98   Some women's voices change during pregnancy and also after giving birth. I've heard contradictory comments about whether being pregnant can assist your singing or cause shortness of breath.

99   If you want to be a professional singer, you have to be highly disciplined. This involves regular vocal training and a strict healthy diet, almost like an athlete.

100   Sing to the end of each phrase. This way it will sound complete and '*legato*'.

101   Singing in your car is very popular but do make sure you don't allow your serious practice to take place when zooming along the motorway!

102   The falsetto is marvellous for accessing the top of your voice. Use this exercise to explore your high notes: imagine you're blowing a trumpet and your cheeks are

full of air. Simply 'blow' a sound out of your mouth like a siren with your lips only slightly apart and pitch as high as you comfortably can on octave leaps.

103 When practising a song, replace the words with random vowel sounds using nonsense syllables. This will enable your jaw to relax and you'll find it easier to produce a good tone.

104 Get in the habit of recording yourself when singing. This will be a huge benefit as you'll be able to hear your voice as others hear you. Remember, the sound you hear in your head is different from what the listener hears.

105 Like learning any new skill, focus on quality of practice rather than quantity.

106 Learning new songs on a regular basis is essential. Don't get stuck singing the same songs all the time. Your voice needs a change.

107 Did you know that the human voice can reach approximately 90dB? Anything above 130dB can cause acute pain and can even burst an eardrum.

108 The loudest insect in the world is the African cicada *(Brevisana brevis)* that produces a song with a level of 106.7dB. The male cicada produces a shrill buzzing sound, vibrating the membranes near the base of the abdomen. Cicada songs play a vital role in their communication and reproduction.

109 We all know that laughing is good for us as it exercises our diaphragm, although too much can upset the

balance of your vocal cords, so be careful, especially before a performance.

110 Some singers open their mouths too wide whilst singing which can cause a breathy tone.

111 The best tone for singing pop music is your natural voice. This is enhanced by the skilful use of breath support and diction.

112 Your singing voice should stem from your 'speaking' voice. Experiment by speaking the words of a song and then sing them as if you're speaking.

113 Manuel Garcia (1805–1906), one of the greatest singing teachers said, "The nose is in the voice but the voice should not be in the nose."

114 Another great teacher, Giovanni Battista Lamperti (1839–1910) said, "The ideal tone is a mouthful of sound that 'spins', remoulds itself for every vowel, is felt on the lips, head, presses down the tongue, pushes up the roof of the mouth, even descends into the chest. In fact, fills every nook and cranny."

115 Are scales a waste of time? No, they help keep the voice toned, flexible and co-ordinated. Singing is a physical activity that improves with adequate and proper preparation.

116 The number one criterion you need in order to improve is to learn to love your voice.

117 When you start singing lessons, decide what you'd like to achieve. Is it a stronger voice? A greater vocal range? To expand your repertoire? Or simply boost your confidence?

118 With written notated music, it can help to imagine the words written above the musical stave rather than below it.

119 It's not ideal to sing and dance at the same time. It's hard to focus on both. You should stand straight and support yourself.

120 Try not to sing with your teeth clenched. This will make your jaw stiff and result in a rigid tone.

121 Act out your song by speaking the words first. This way you'll get to grips with the real meaning of the words and become good at communicating the message of the song.

122 If you're asked to sing at a concert, you'll need plenty of preparation time. Whatever you do, don't leave it to the last minute.

123 Your voice is not separate from the rest of your body. The impulse to communicate with your voice is a natural thing. Your voice is affected by the environment, your relationship with yourself and with other people.

124 What's meant by the 'timbre' of the voice? It's the actual quality of the sound or tone.

125 The 'Vaccai' is series of progressive singing exercises, in Italian, which help the singer with pitching intervals, ornamentation and legato singing.

126 Tongue-twisters are good fun to practise, especially if you're serious about being on stage e.g. "Bibby's baubles glisten gloriously like glossy glass."

127 Listening to Mozart is said to improve one's brain power because of his particular melodic architecture and the way in which tunes are developed. Singing Mozart is also very challenging and excellent discipline for young singers.

128 What's meant by 'pacing a song'? This is when you think through the entire song, knowing where the highs and lows are. It's no good peaking too soon as you'll have nowhere to go if another climax is required.

129 What's meant by *'passaggio'* or 'break'? This is when there's a noticeable change in gear in the voice. Most singers have distinct changes in sound at certain pitches which need to be smoothed out by the singing teacher.

130 Always work on your 'head' voice. This can help smooth out register 'breaks' and offer a wider range and variety of sounds available.

131 Slouching inhibits your breath control and makes your body work harder than necessary.

132 Did you know that singing can help improve snoring? Singing tones the muscles of the throat, particularly the soft palate and this helps keep the airway open and reduces the 'rattle' sound.

133 In order to help you extend long notes, imagine the breath is like a jet-stream and there is a ping pong ball on top.

134 Singing helps people in the workplace communicate on a new level. Making music together provides a shared motivational experience and is now hugely popular in the corporate arena as team-building events.

135 Singing makes you feel happy because endorphins are released into the body.

136 Learning to sing at a young age is excellent as it helps with concentration and co-ordination.

137 Singing is also good for promoting self-discipline, as regular practice is required if you want to improve.

Health Tips

138 Singing is actually gentle aerobic exercise and it helps tone the muscles of the face and stomach.

139 Did you know that regular singing can help you look younger? We can forget those expensive anti-ageing creams now!

140 Avoid air-conditioning as it can cause dehydration.

141 Regular singing will keep your voice in good shape, so make sure you follow a good warm-up routine and do this at the same time each day.

142 Drink at least 10 glasses of still water to keep your voice in top condition.

143 If you're performing outdoors it's important to take extra care of your voice and body. Try not to eat for two hours before a performance, so that your diaphragm can expand to its fullest.

144 Be kind to your voice by not talking for extended periods of time.

145 Do practise singing by watching yourself in a mirror. The saying goes, "If it looks right, it'll sound right."

146 Avoid strenuous exercise at least two hours before singing. It displaces your larynx.

147 When you next sing a song, try closing your eyes and see what a difference it makes to your sound and imagination. It works wonders.

148 To avoid being too rigid when singing, walk around the room and swing your arms freely.

149 Did you know that the intense physical effort involved in singing properly can result in weight loss? Singers who perform demanding operatic roles will regularly lose pounds overnight, while putting on muscle long term.

150 However overweight or underweight you are, you can still have a great singing voice. You don't need to be fat in order to sing opera as some people think!

151 Singing is a type of sport and is more fun than running on the treadmill. One hour of singing could help you burn approximately 200–400 calories, depending on your age, weight and body fat.

152 Every muscle in your body, if tightened, can affect muscles in the throat. By contrast, controlling the voice muscles has the effect of easing tension throughout the body.

153 In hot weather, ice-cold drinks are soothing, but they are a disaster for a singer because they tighten up the vocal cords, which must be warm and loose in order to sing properly.

154 Cheering and screaming at outdoor sporting events, such as football matches, is not conducive to good voice

care. It can leave you with a sore throat or, worse still, irreparable damage.

155 Avoid electric fans to keep you cool in the hot summer. Constant air being blown into your face can set off a sore throat.

156 If you have tension around the larynx area, where your vocal cords are situated, this can reduce the width of your throat, leaving less resonance in your voice. Learn how to relax.

157 Oral hygiene is highly important for a singer, so remember to brush your teeth at least twice if not three times a day.

158 You may also want to consider brushing your tongue as well to get rid of any stains or residue.

159 On the subject of teeth, ensure you visit your dentist at least twice a year. If you're on TV, you may want to discuss the option of teeth-whitening.

160 Don't worry if you salivate whilst singing, it's a good sign. Your mouth should be moist so keep drinking the H2O.

161 A singer's body is his or her own instrument. Make sure you give your voice and body the proper rest it deserves.

162 Good vocal training works the 'core' muscles of the body and it's not a bad thing to build up a sweat whilst singing. Some trained singers find the abs machine at their gym relatively easy as their abdomen is a well-developed area of the body.

163 When speaking on the phone, ensure that you don't twist your head at an angle in order to speak. This can cause a strain on your voice. Focus on what's happening to your body. Sit up straight or stand up whilst on the phone.

164 Avoid clothing that's too tight around your middle or neck, e.g. a belt, tie, scarf or heavy jewellery.

165 Singing is a good way for older or disabled people to reap the benefits of gentle aerobic exercise.

166 Singing uses more of your lung capacity than normal, which oxygenates the blood and helps with circulation. How healthy is that!

Karaoke Tips

167 Singing at karaoke is a great means of relaxing and switching off from work or daily routine. It can make you feel rejuvenated afterwards.

168 When you sing at karaoke, the chances are you might be nervous to begin with. Focus on the meaning of the words and not on yourself. This will help you relax and look more confident.

169 "I've never gotten over what they call stage fright. I go through it every show." Elvis Presley

170 When we're nervous our voices tend to go higher in pitch and we sing faster than normal. Allow yourself to slow down by breathing deeply and evenly.

171 Take your time before you begin a song. Never feel rushed.

172 Singing with a microphone is different from singing without one. If you use one, be aware that you don't need as much abdominal support as normal. You should also stand back slightly when you have to sing with more volume.

173 The good news about karaoke is that you can change the key of the song to suit your voice.

174 Choose a song you know really well. You'll probably have the support of your friends to help you relax plus there'll be a cue so you can follow the words easily.

175 Don't take it too seriously! The main aim is to have fun and let your hair down.

176 Sing for fun and sing because you love it. It's great to share your voice with the world.

177 It's wonderful to celebrate every accomplishment no matter how small.

"God gave me a voice to sing with, and when you have that, what other gimmick is there?" Whitney Houston

Autumn

Some dos and don'ts

General Singing Tips

178 If you can hear your inhalation, you're probably taking in too much air. Your breath should be inaudible.

179 In order to have a beautiful resonance, vibrate your voice on the hard palate of your mouth.

180 When approaching a high note, open your arms and imagine you're able to make the note bigger with your own hands. This'll create an opening effect and enable you to sing the high note easily.

181 Yodelling is when the voice quickly alters between the chest register into head voice, and back into chest again.

182 Each person's bone structure has a profound impact on the quality of their singing voice. This is because areas of resonance are in the face and head.

183 Eye focus is important when singing and can be distracting to the audience. Focus on an imaginary spot at the back of the room, a few feet above you.

184 There are several terms synonymous with phrasing. These are 'line', '*legato*' and '*sostenuto*' Italian for 'sustaining'. They refer to a smooth and flowing tone.

185 Did you know that every note you sing has its own unique setting of the vocal cords?

186 Belting is when your voice is dominated by the chest register, which sounds raw and loud. It's used in musical theatre singing and must be used with caution.

187 Vocal problems usually begin if you sing under stressful conditions and you're not getting enough rest.

188 Today we rely so much on social media that the art of communicating with others verbally is decreasing. Allow yourself to speak or sing whenever you can.

189 You'll gain power in your voice by strengthening the muscles in your ribcage and back.

190 Singing is a holistic experience and can help you get in touch with your emotions.

191 A baby is able to cry and cry and not get tired whereas a fan at a football match will not be able to speak the following day after screaming and shouting. This is because the baby has no inhibitions and is using his/her diaphragm freely.

192 When singing, put a finger under your chin. If the skin is loose, your tongue is probably relaxed and in an ideal

position. If it's hard and tense, you're less likely to produce a good tone.

193 According to some schools of thought, getting in touch with your breath allows you to get in touch with your sexuality.

194 What's a 'torch' song? This is a sultry ballad in jazz which has a slow burning quality usually sung by women. It's best not to try and make your voice sound husky though.

195 Aeroplane travel is usually terrible for singers as cabin air is dry and can irritate the mucus membranes on your cords. Drink plenty of water or juice and avoid alcohol. Cabins are also deceptively noisy, so don't talk too much.

196 *Colla voce* in music means the singer is free to take some liberty with the timing, usually for one bar of music.

197 A trill is a small vocal embellishment that usually involves two notes being sung rapidly and alternately for a specific length. Classical songs of the baroque era use this feature.

198 The interval of the 4th is difficult for the voice to pitch, both ascending and descending. Therefore, it's good to work on.

199 Scat singing is a free form of improvisation used in jazz. Listen, for example, to Cleo Laine, a great exponent of this.

200 Who were the *'castrati'*? They were male singers in church choirs originally from Italy, who were castrated

before reaching puberty in order to keep their voices sounding young. At the time women's voices weren't allowed in church. Castrati also appeared in opera throughout the 17th and 18th centuries. They had disappeared from the operatic stage by the 1820s, though not from the Vatican choir until a century later.

201 How do you know your range? Usually you can tell by a singer's speaking voice, otherwise your teacher will explore this with you during lessons by doing various vocal exercises and listening to where the best timbre of your voice is.

202 Some singers feel intimidated if they have to speak to an audience. Believe it or not, the audience enjoy hearing you speak!

203 Depending on the kind of song you're singing, you may want to ensure you pronounce the ends of words clearly. It's frustrating hearing only part of a word, especially in classical music.

204 If you've developed a proper technique, you should be able to sing in various positions whether sitting or lying down.

205 No doubt you'll benefit from going to live performances as well as listening to your iPod and watching different singers on YouTube.

206 What's the best way to tackle a new song? If a recording is available, hear it. There may be several versions so it's good to compare. If not, then read through the song as if you're an actor preparing lines for a play. Then look at the melody line. Don't try and do everything at once.

207 As the colder months approach, a lot of singers take fitness classes indoors. This is OK as long as you don't sing immediately afterwards.

208 What's a vocal lick? This is where the voice plays around with a certain vocal inflection or ornamentation. It's used in jazz singing.

209 Singing can help overcome shyness.

210 Some singers are able to sight-read which means they're able to sing from a notated score the first time they see the music with no preparation. If you practice reading music daily, you can improve your sight-reading skills.

211 In German, the word '*Sprechstimme*' (speak voice) indicates halfway between talking and singing. It's indicated by an 'x' sign.

212 Above the falsetto is the flageolet or whistle register that some voices have. It's extremely high and some children are able to access this without any effort.

213 The most popular type of microphone is cordless. If you're using your own ensure that you've got spare batteries as they can run out quickly.

214 In musical theatre singing, you'd be given a head mike which is usually pinned onto your head under a wig.

215 What determines a great voice? Like all instruments, human voice quality is determined by resonance. The fundamental vibration of the vocal cords becomes beautiful by the addition of desirable harmonics. Some of these are determined by the shape and density of the teeth, jaw and sinuses, and by the singer's pharynx, the

part of the throat at the back of the mouth. Presumably those with a naturally pleasant singing voice have a lucky coincidence of skeleton and pharyngeal shape.

216   There may be several reasons why someone can't sing well even if they can sing in tune. It's to do with the range of frequencies produced by their vocal cords. Some may not be able to achieve sufficient control over their larynx or tongue and in some cases the vibrations of the vocal cords may be irregular. Sometimes the cords can't close correctly or they may be too dry to function properly.

217   Why do some people sing out of tune? Inaccurate tuning or pitching is a problem that every singer will experience at some stage. The main reasons are bad breathing, not listening correctly or tiredness.

218   Be careful when singing words that begin or end with the letter 'S'. Ensure it's not too sibilant and becomes 'Ssss'. When the tip of the tongue is brought near the roof of the mouth and air is pushed past the tongue, it makes a hissing sound.

219   The opposite problem is the 'aspirate' attack, in which excessive air is released prior to phonation, i.e. producing a sound. While this type of attack rarely damages the vocal cords, it causes a breathy tone quality.

220   The voice will eventually begin to deteriorate. You can delay this process by taking great care of your voice.

221   Flare your nostrils when you breathe in; this will help lift and engage your soft palate, which is essential for producing a good sound.

222 What's perfect pitch? This is when you can pitch any named note and sing it. It's a gift if you're sight-reading, but in some situations can be a hindrance, e.g. when singing baroque music which is usually at period (lower) pitch.

223 Opera singers have a lot of muscle on their body, especially around the middle and the neck area, whereas most pop singers are usually thin.

224 It's been suggested that singing prolongs life! According to research in the U.S., choral singing increases life expectancy, because regular singing in groups improves your mood and keeps your heart healthy.

225 Singing is a therapeutic activity and is finding its way into numerous areas of healthcare, with studies showing that it helps breathing problems, stress-related illnesses, depression, dementia, snoring and the immune system.

226 Learning to sing with real feeling requires a brave willingness to allow others to hear your innermost thoughts.

227 Environmental conditions such as dryness, dampness, cold, dust, smoke, pollution and noise, all affect your voice especially as the weather gets colder.

Dos

228 Did you know that singing is at least 80% confidence? If you believe you can do it, you will. Think positively, and you'll achieve your goals.

229 Sing from the deepest place in your body. Anchor your sound in the pit of your stomach and you'll connect with your inner emotions.

230 Visualisation is a powerful tool for creating results. Imagine a physical space both above and below any singing note. This will help create an infinite sound. Your audience should never be aware of where your voice begins and ends.

231 It's okay to show your teeth when singing, but make sure you don't purse your lips.

232 Switching your usual style of singing is very freeing and will give you an idea of other disciplines and open up your mind.

233 Tea and coffee are full of caffeine so it's best to avoid them. Try herbal or fruit teas instead.

234 If your throat isn't in good shape, rest! That means no singing or speaking.

235 The tongue is a powerful muscle and some singers have problems with it. For example, rising up on certain notes which obstructs the sound. Try stretching out your tongue as far as possible for a few seconds.

236 Practise these consonants: P, D, K, G and B. Ensure air doesn't escape.

237 Also, M, N, L, R, V and W are sung consonants and good to practise on various pitches.

238 You can't rush learning to sing. Practise slowly, especially when starting a new song.

239 "The beautiful thing about learning is that no one can take it away from you." B.B. King

240 If you're in vocal difficulty during your aria or song it could be because your throat is getting tight. An easy way out of this is to keep the tongue forward, slightly over the bottom teeth.

241 It can help to stand up in order to sing high notes.

242 When aiming for high or low notes, imagine going in the opposite direction. When going up high, think low, and vice versa.

243 "Am I afraid of high notes? Of course I'm afraid. What sane man isn't?" Luciano Pavarotti

244 Try bending your knees as you sing up high. This will help to anchor you.

245 Children do most things with ease, so get in touch with your inner child and sing with joy and freedom.

246 "Man becomes that which he gazes upon." George Harrison

Don'ts

247 Don't ever blast out the beginning of a phrase, even if it says '*ff*' (*fortissimo*). Grow into it gently.

248 Avoid using the term 'hitting' notes. In my view it's preferable to say 'reaching', which is much kinder.

249 If you wear reading glasses when singing, make sure this doesn't cause you either to throw back your head or pull your chin down as this could affect your larynx.

250 Don't pull your head down whilst singing, as this causes the ribs to slump towards the stomach, making the chest narrow. The voice would then sound monotonous.

251 Conversely, raising your head too high and sticking out your rear, will cause the voice to sound pinched and forced.

252 Some singers gesticulate when singing. Don't overdo it. If it feels natural and is part of the expression, fine.

253 Don't allow yourself to be led by your accompanist. Often singers wait for a signal and don't have the confidence to lead. Just do it!

254 If you're a soprano, then don't sing alto, and if you're a tenor, it's no good singing bass. Stick with the range that shows you off best.

255 Some singers have an annoying habit of nodding or blinking in time to the music. I'm afraid it looks naff and unprofessional. Watch yourself in the mirror or get feedback from someone else.

256 Be careful not to sweep up to notes. It's irritating when singers constantly approach the sound from below. Aim to sing from above.

257 It's not recommended that a young male singer starts lessons whilst his voice is breaking, i.e. the change during puberty when the vocal cords naturally extend. It's best to wait at least six months after the voice has 'broken'.

258 Never sing to the point of vocal exhaustion. This will not result in a stronger or higher singing range; it'll

have the opposite effect. Remember, your voice is you and needs to be well looked-after.

259 If a song is out of your vocal range or is too big for your voice type, don't sing it. There are plenty of others to choose from.

260 Apart from dairy produce, other foods to avoid before a performance or singing lesson include hot or spicy foods, nuts, crisps or any foods which may get stuck in your throat.

261 Drugs are not good for the vocal cords as they can damage the cartilage of your larynx.

262 Remember, we do have to think technically when singing in performance rather than get carried away with the drama.

263 Avoid speaking in noisy places, as this'll put a strain on your voice.

264 Ladies, don't share lipsticks! They carry germs!

265 Don't stop to listen and check every single note as this can inhibit the natural flow of a phrase. This is when you need another pair of trusted ears to listen.

"Ability may get you to the top, but it takes character to keep you there." Stevie Wonder

Winter

Includes audition tips and performance tips

General Singing Tips

266   During winter, we sometimes need a pick-me-up as some people suffer from 'seasonal affective disorder' or SAD. Singing has the power to uplift the soul and make us feel good. Your health will benefit too.

267   If you get sick and have a sore throat, don't bother with throat lozenges as they have a drying effect on the voice. Have ordinary sweets instead or a soft drink.

268   If your voice is tired, try using a steam inhaler. You don't need to add anything to the water, just inhale deeply and allow your throat to be soothed. For best results, do this for a minimum of five minutes.

269   How would you know if you've pushed your voice? Usually it'll hurt and feel strained. This is the time you need to stop.

270 In icy weather it's best not to talk, let alone sing. It's very hard on your lungs and throat. Again, look after your health as you are number 1.

271 Natural remedies like honey and lemon are excellent for the throat.

272 Another remedy for a sore throat is to gargle with salted warm water. This can help reduce swelling.

273 Central heating isn't great for the body, skin or voice. If you can avoid it, do.

274 Germs spread quickly in warm centrally heated places, so ensure that you wash your hands frequently so as not to pass germs to your nose and mouth.

275 If you have to sing when you're unwell, try and avoid throat sprays, talk as little as possible and drink warm herbal teas.

276 Having a 'head' cold can sometimes be an advantage as it helps focus the sound in the resonators, i.e. the mouth, nose and throat.

277 Ladies, it's preferable to wear low instead of high heels. This way, your body weight will be evenly balanced; you'll breathe better and therefore sing better.

278 Avoid 'throat clearing' or coughing. This is bad for the vocal cords, as they grate together like sandpaper.

279 It's good to give your cheeks a little massage when singing as it will help relax the muscles in the face.

280 Keep your voice as pure as possible. *Vibrato* can develop later in your training.

281 A lot of people enjoy singing in the shower because the resonance is fantastic, due to bathroom tiles which allow your voice to bounce around. So, wherever you're singing, imagine you're in the shower!

282 Be careful not to open your mouth too wide when singing. Your jaw should be comfortably open.

283 Imagine you're inhaling or drinking back your own singing voice. The Italians say '*inhalare la voce*' which means to inhale the voice.

284 Keep a humidifier in your room at night as this'll help keep your cords hydrated.

285 An excellent warm-up exercise is to sing 'Ma ma ma ma ma' (up five notes on a scale) and then 'Ma ma ma ma ma' (descend on the same notes). You can start this in the middle register ascending in semitones on each set.

286 Try opening your eyes wide when you sing. Showing your eyeballs helps elevate the palate which then improves the sound.

287 I'm often asked how to get a bigger sound. The best way is by using your diaphragm muscle correctly. Don't ever force your throat.

288 It's best to avoid using your chest voice in the higher register. It should be used sparingly and for special effects only.

289 If you normally produce rich, free-flowing vowels in exercises and then suddenly experience a thin, unwanted huskiness when singing, your consonants are probably too strong.

290 As you take emphasis away from consonants, you'll have to put greater reliance on the vowels. You should learn to add strength via the support muscles to vowels after the consonant. If you don't, the line of vowels will sound weak.

291 When you sing in a 'dry' room, i.e. without any reverberation or feedback, be careful not to force your voice.

292 What's a covered tone? This is when the voice sounds muffled and unclear and is characterised by a darker quality.

293 What's a nodule? This is a wart on your vocal cords. They prevent your cords from working correctly.

294 If you have nodules this might be as a result of singing badly. Surgery should be your last resort. In some cases, you may be advised by your laryngologist not to speak for several weeks!

295 Avoid singing at your loudest for extended periods of time.

296 Singing is not only a release of energy but also a transformation of energy and supports our wholeness as human beings.

297 Own your song. This means putting your interpretation on the music, words and expressions and not copying someone else.

298 What's *coloratura*? This refers to florid and flexible singing of fast passages, often up high. Beverly Sills and Joan Sutherland were *coloratura* experts!

299 If you've trouble learning a *cadenza* or long passage, try singing it from the last note first. Sing the last few notes over and over until you've got it. Then still working from the end of the *cadenza*, add a few more notes and so on. This is a great way to get it into your voice.

300 It's a myth that singing early in the morning isn't a good idea. Often people get tense and stressed during the working day, so by evening they're in no fit state to sing. Try an early morning singing session!

301 Singing can help people suffering from depression to gain control and to understand how their voice reflects their inner self.

302 The colour green is said to represent the heart area so if you're singing a love ballad, think green and see what happens....

303 To help expand your breath, hold the last note of a phrase for as long as possible. See how many seconds you can manage, then repeat. This time expand your ribs and don't collapse your chest. Feel the breath making your back grow; if you focus on a spot on the wall it can help.

304 If you take sleeping tablets it can cause your voice to dry out, so find a herbal alternative.

305 Research in Sweden has shown that choir singers not only harmonise their voices, they also synchronise their heartbeats.

306 Relying on sheet music or a music score if you know the music, is cheating. My advice is to come away from the score as soon as possible.

307 It's good to practice when you're alone in a comfortable environment without the fear of interruptions or unwelcome comments from family members or neighbours.

308 No doubt there'll be times when your voice just won't do what you want it to. It's best to leave it alone and come back later.

309 Focus on setting realistic goals with your singing. You may wish to learn a certain number of songs each month or sing in public every so often or even work towards putting on a concert. Whatever it is, write it down and work towards it.

310 Positive thinking really does make a huge difference to your general well-being and your singing.

311 "I want to make my voice work in the same way as a trombone or violin, i.e. to 'play' the voice like an instrument." Frank Sinatra

Audition Tips

312 Auditions are not easy. Always be yourself and remember that the panel are just as human as you are. Treat it like you're giving an encore performance.

313 Be careful when considering your songs. It's no good bringing along complicated piano parts, because your pianist may mess up your performance. Either take your

own pianist to an audition, which can be costly, choose simpler songs, or sometimes you can send your music to the audition panel in advance.

314 Take at least three contrasting pieces even though they may only ask for one. Be prepared to be stopped at any time and don't be offended by this.

315 Please don't use a backing track in an audition.

316 Do your homework thoroughly! Be prepared by knowing all your songs from memory and take along extra copies of the music in case you're asked for it.

317 Make sure your music is clearly marked with any vocal nuances, e.g. repeats, cuts, edits, pauses, crescendos/decrescendos and breath marks.

318 There's a chance you may be asked what your range is. Be honest, as you could be required to demonstrate this.

319 Ensure you take along an up-to-date CV together with a recent photograph, preferably a head and shoulders shot. Do invest in some professional photographs, as the panel don't want happy family portraits. Also, put your name and contact details on the back of the photo.

320 Always be polite and professional.

Performance Tips

321 There's a saying "If you don't practise for one day, you'll know it. If you don't practise for two days, the critics will know it. If you don't practise for three days, the public will know it."

322 "I learned you have to trust yourself, be what you are, and do what you ought to do the way you should do it. You have got to discover what you do, and trust it." Barbra Streisand

323 It's a good idea to seek out professional advice from several trusted sources before embarking on a singing career.

324 Sorry to say that it's a myth that a glass of port will warm and lubricate your vocal cords. You should avoid alcohol when performing.

325 What's the underlying message of your chosen song? Is there a subtext? Is it a love song or a sad song? Are you telling a story? Understand the message of any song before you perform it.

326 "Music is a shorthand to emotion." Leo Tolstoy

327 This may seem obvious, but ensure that your hair is not in your face when singing. The audience wants to see your eyes!

328 When warming-up your voice with exercises before a performance, it's best to start with the lower register.

329 When using a microphone, treat it as if it were your best friend. Be kind and gentle with it.

330 A professional performer's lifestyle can be a huge strain, e.g. eating late at night, doing the same thing for weeks on end and having disrupted sleeping patterns. You must take extra care and eat healthy foods as much as possible.

331 It's an acquired skill to transpose songs and can take some preparation and training. Don't expect someone to be able to do this perfectly at the last minute.

332 Being in the right place at the right time is certainly helpful in any singer's career. Ensure you allow yourself plenty of opportunities to network.

333 Take advantage of performing opportunities. This'll boost your confidence and give you something to work towards.

334 When nervous, the adrenalin kicks in, which is normal. Use it as fuel for your singing.

335 Singing at gigs, recording sessions or band rehearsals shouldn't be considered practice. You must make time for yourself to sing without the pressure of having to sound good or perform for other people.

336 Singers get scared at the thought of harmonising with others. The more often you do it, the better you'll become.

337 Ensure you can summarise your song in a simple sentence. Your performance will then have some meaning.

338 Before you give a performance, think about what you'll be wearing. Do your clothes reflect the mood of the song? Keep a note of what you wear and when.

339 You can mentally practise a performance by visualising yourself doing it. See it going well.

340 The difference between singing in a studio and on stage in front of an audience is that in a studio you're likely to

do lots of stopping and starting, whereas on stage you sing right through without any re-takes. The pressures are different so you'll need to get used to both.

341 Don't panic if your voice is hoarse when you first wake up. It doesn't mean this is how you'll sound in the evening. It can take a while for your voice to wake up too.

342 To help you relax before a performance have a cup of camomile tea or put a few drops of lavender oil on an item of clothing you're wearing.

343 On the day of a performance, you'll need as much rest as possible. A brief warm-up in the morning is good followed by a more intense 20 minutes a couple of hours before the performance. You'll find what works best for you the more experience you get.

344 If you're a professional singer, I recommend having a website. The resources available to you online are considerable.

345 On the day of a performance it's ok to be entirely selfish. Nothing takes priority except you giving 100% to your singing.

346 Mindfulness meditation is an excellent way to recharge your batteries before any major performance.

347 If you have any self-doubt (which all human beings experience at some point) I suggest doing some positive affirmations every morning. Read them aloud and watch yourself in the mirror whilst doing this. The rule is to be consistent. It's great to remind yourself how truly wonderful you are.

348 It's normal to be nervous when singing in front of others. Take a few deep breaths before starting and focus on the message and meaning of the song.

349 After a performance it's still important to take care of your voice.

350 Share your gift with others. Everyone in your audience wants you to sing for them.

351 The human voice is the most precious gift ever. It transcends any other musical instrument and should be treated with the utmost love, care and respect.

More famous tips

352 "I think of myself as a performance artist. I hate being called a pop star." Madonna

353 "I'm always doing that which I cannot do, in order that I may learn how to do it." Pablo Picasso

354 "It's not only by yielding to one's impulses that one achieves greatness, but also by patiently filing away the steel wall that separates what one feels one is capable of doing." Vincent Van Gogh

355 "It's odd how the creative power at once brings the whole universe to order." Virginia Woolf

356 "When you're content to be simply yourself and don't compare and compete, everyone will respect you." Old Chinese proverb from Tao Te Ching

357 "Keep away from people who try to belittle your ambitions. Small people always do that, but the really

great make you feel that you too can become great." Mark Twain

358 "Our deepest fear is not that we are inadequate, it is that we are powerful beyond measure." Marianne Williamson/Nelson Mandela

359 "If you can walk you can dance, if you talk you can sing." Zimbabwean saying

360 "You must be the change you wish to see in the world." Mahatma Gandhi

361 "Before you can move their tears, your own must flow. To convince them you yourself must believe." Winston Churchill

362 "Rivers know this: there is no hurry, we shall get there some day." Winnie the Pooh

363 "Success is a science. If you have the right conditions you get the results." Oscar Wilde

364 "Always bear in mind that your own resolution to succeed is more important than any one thing." Abraham Lincoln

365 "Most of the shadows of life are caused by us standing in our own sunshine" Ralph Waldo Emerson

♫

4862038R00036

Printed in Great Britain
by Amazon.co.uk, Ltd.,
Marston Gate.